LANDFORMS

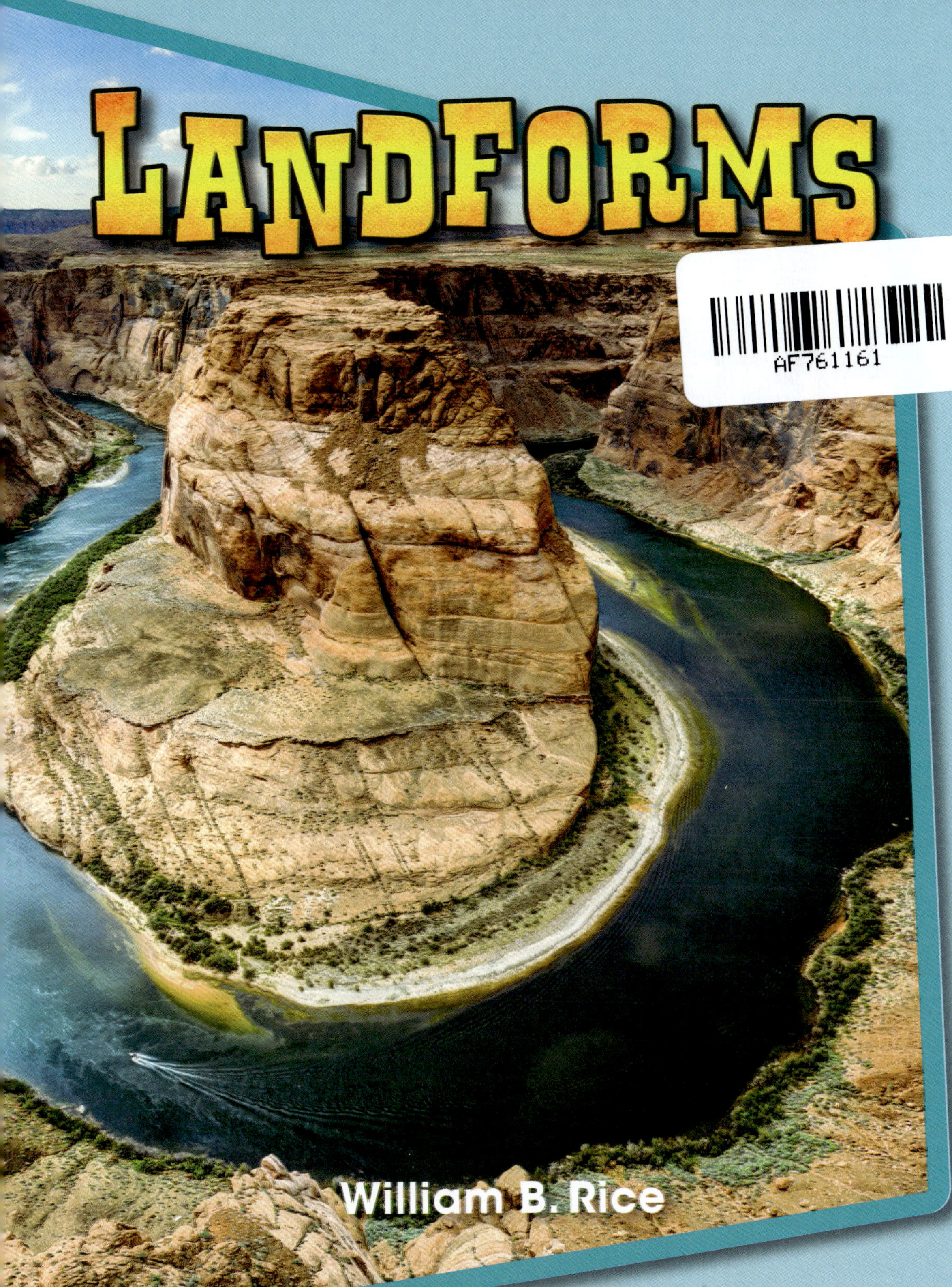

William B. Rice

Consultants

Sally Creel, Ed.D.
Curriculum Consultant

Leann Iacuone, M.A.T., NBCT, ATC
Riverside Unified School District

Image Credits: pp.18 (top), 20 (top) NASA; 19 (top) Norman Kuring/NASA; p.28–29 (illustrations) Janelle Bell-Martin; p.10 Luca Galuzzi/wiki; all other images from Shutterstock.

Library of Congress Cataloging-in-Publication Data

Rice, William B. (William Benjamin), 1961- author.
Landforms / William B. Rice ; consultants, Sally Creel, Ed.D., curriculum consultant, Leann Iacuone, M.A.T., NBCT, ATC, Riverside Unified School District, Jill Tobin, California Teacher of the Year semi-finalist, Burbank Unified School District.
pages cm
Audience: K to grade 3.
Includes index.
ISBN 978-1-4807-4608-4 (pbk.)
ISBN 978-1-4807-5075-3 (ebook)
1. Landforms—Juvenile literature.
2. Earth (Planet)—Juvenile literature. I. Title.
GB404.R53 2015
551.3—dc23

2014014115

Teacher Created Materials
5301 Oceanus Drive
Huntington Beach, CA 92649-1030
http://www.tcmpub.com

ISBN 978-1-4807-4608-4

Printed by: 51497
Printed in: China

Table of Contents

Our Beautiful Earth

We live on a stunning planet. Everywhere we look, the land has many beauties.

The land also has many shapes. Each shape has a charm of its own. There are flat shapes and bumpy shapes. There are high places and low places. There are places with water and places without water.

Each of these forms is like no other. Each is one of Earth's many landforms.

Some land has much less water than other land.

The Big Picture

If we look at a map or a photo of Earth, we can easily see the biggest landforms.

Oceans are the large bodies of water that cover most of Earth's surface. There are five of them. Between the oceans, there are big masses of land. There are seven in all. These are the continents.

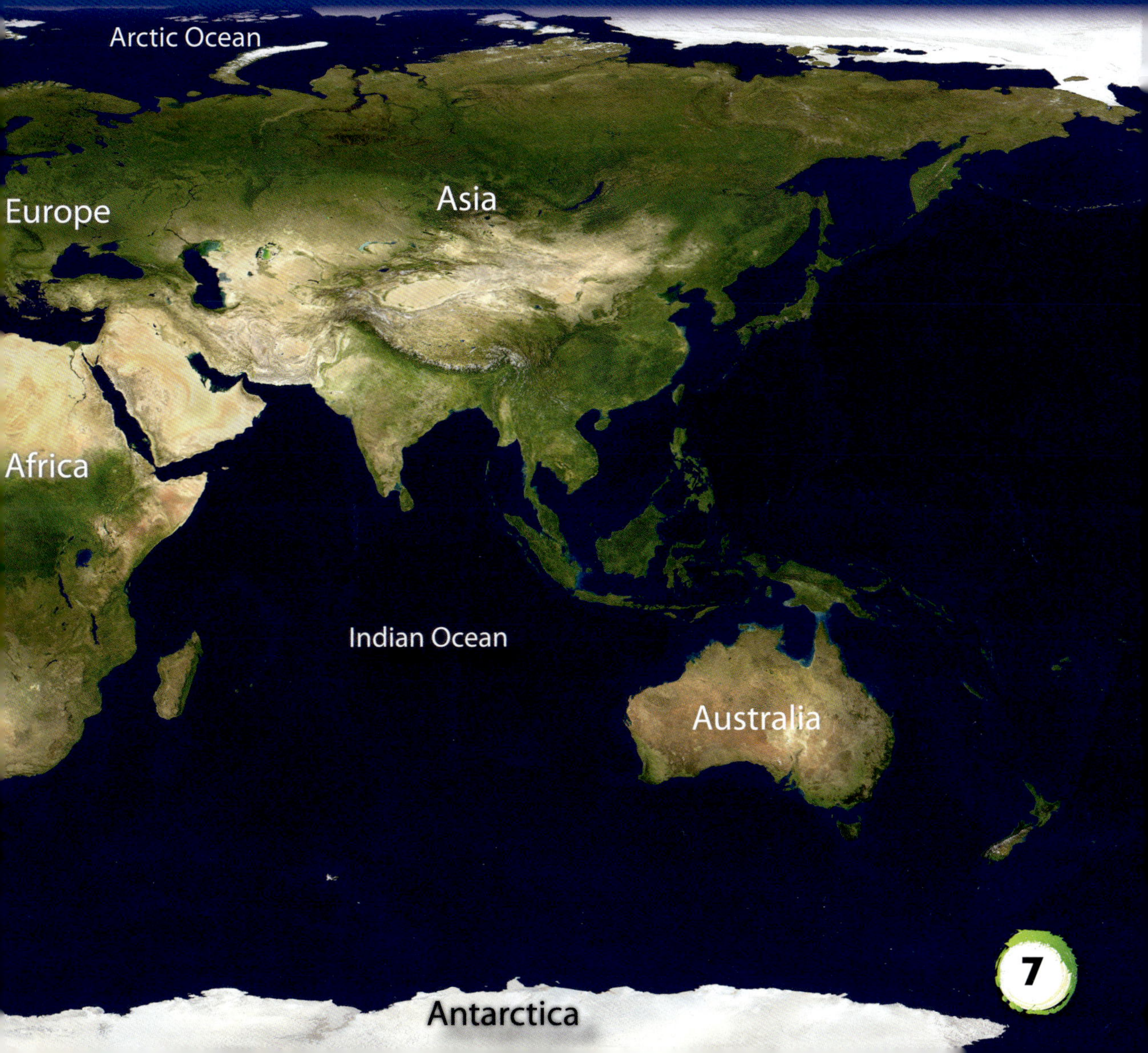

Describing Landforms

Land has many different shapes. So, people have a word for each shape. These words tell us about the landform. They tell us how big or how high it is.

The tallest mountain is Mount Everest.

Elevation tells how high something is. **Slope** tells how **steep** the sides are.

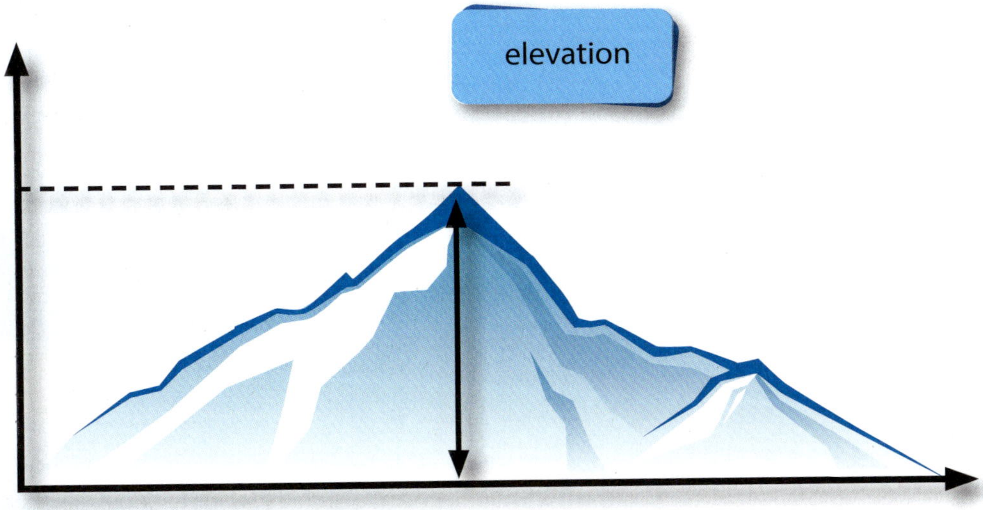

The Atlas Mountains have a desert climate.

Climate

There are many things that affect landforms. The amount of rain and snow that a place gets affects them. How hot or cold they get also affects them. So does how wet or dry they get.

The usual weather for a place is called its **climate**. Some parts of Earth get more or less of these things than others. There are many different climates around the world.

The Atlas Mountains are in Africa.

Deep Earth Processes

Deep Earth processes are things that happen deep inside Earth. Over long periods of time, these events help create most of the landforms we see.

On Land

Many landforms in the world are above ground, so they can be seen easily.

Mountains and Hills

When we look at the land, we may see places that are very high compared to the rest of the land. These are mountains. The tops of mountains are called **peaks**. Mountains usually have steep slopes.

Rolling hills are not as steep as the Himalayas.

Then again, we might see places that are higher than the surrounding area but not as high as mountains. Their sides may not be as steep, either. These are hills.

The highest mountains on Earth are called the *Himalayas*. They are in Asia.

Ice Caps

In some areas on Earth, the land is covered by ice. These are ice caps. In these areas, we can only see the very tops of mountains.

Plateaus and Mesas

Sometimes, there are high areas of land that are mainly flat. They are **plateaus** (pla-TOHZ). Their name is a French word that means “table land.”

Colorado Plateau in North America

Some forms with flat tops stick up in the middle of other flat areas. These are mesas. They look like tables. In fact, *mesa* is the Spanish word for *table*.

Tibetan Plateau in Asia

Canyons and Valleys

Landforms in low areas may have high, flat walls of rock around them. There are steep sides between the low and high areas. The sides may be straight up and down in some parts. They form cliffs. These areas are **canyons**.

Grand Canyon

The Grand Canyon in Arizona is one of the most famous canyons in the world.

Low, flat places may be surrounded by the slopes of mountains and hills. These slopes may be steep or gentle. These are valleys. Valleys are not as deep as canyons.

Kalalau Valley, Hawaii

On the Edge

Some landforms mark the place between land and sea. They seem to be on the edge of land.

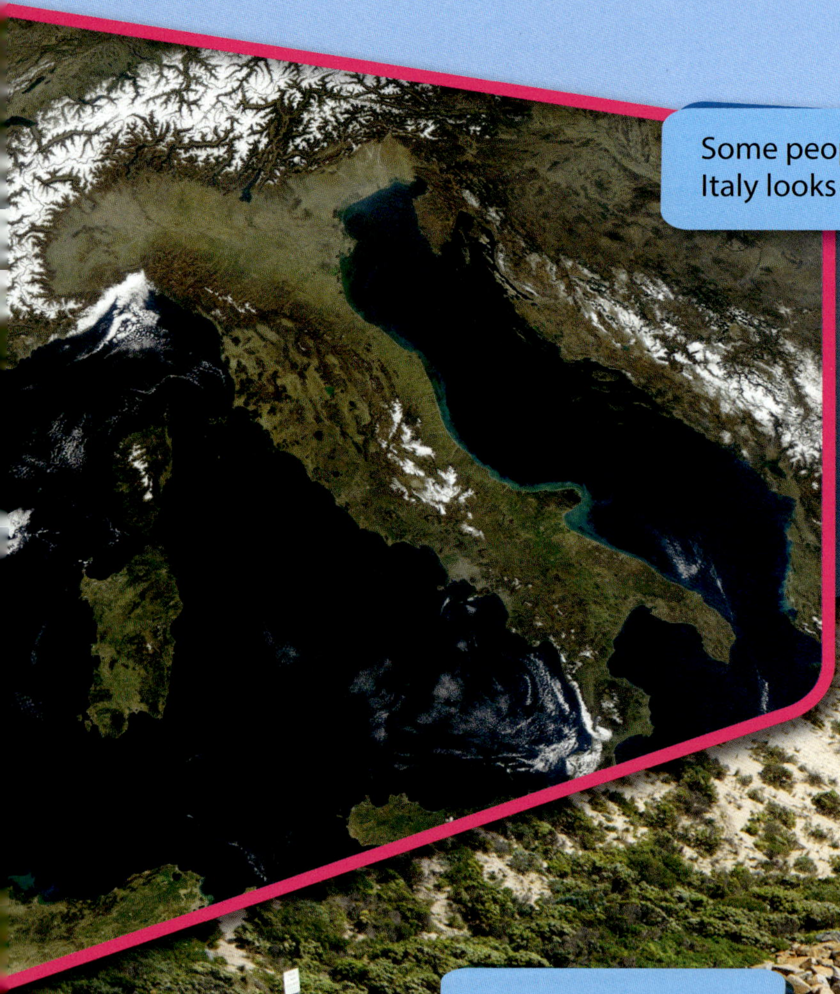

Some people say that Italy looks like a boot!

a beach in Australia

Coastlines and Peninsulas

All around the world, oceans and land meet. The coastline is where they touch. The land may be long and flat with a lot of sand. This is called a *beach*.

In some places, we find long pieces of land surrounded by water on all but one side. The land looks like a finger sticking into the water. This is called a *peninsula*. Its name means "almost island."

the Baja Peninsula

Bays and Gulfs

On a map of Earth, we see small parts of ocean surrounded on many sides by land. These are bays. Bays are usually small and have calm waters. Gulfs are just like bays, but they are larger.

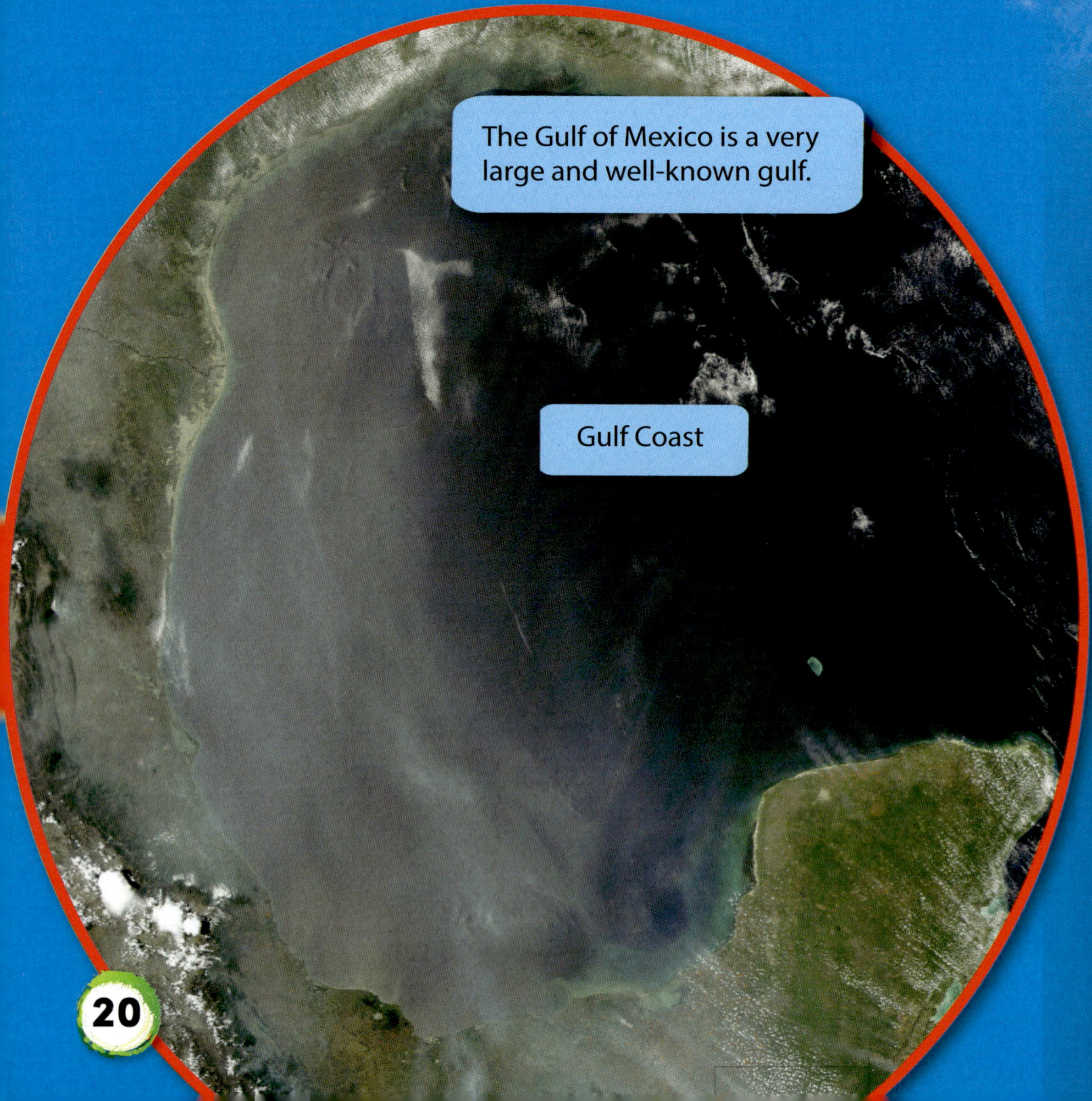

Mission Bay in San Diego, California

Bay of Bengal near India

Seas

Another large body of water is a sea. Sometimes, *sea* is used in place of *ocean*. But they are not the same thing. Seas are smaller than oceans. They are partially blocked in by land. Seas are not as calm as bays and gulfs.

The Sea of Japan is northwest of Japan.

The South China Sea is between Vietnam and the Philippines.

Sea of Japan

Under the Sea

Landforms are everywhere. They are even at the bottom of the oceans!

Oceans and Mid-Ocean Ridges

Oceans are very, very deep. But there is still land beneath them! There are hills and valleys. There are even long chains of underwater mountains. They are called mid-ocean **ridges**. Some of these chains are so tall that they reach above water! There are also extra deep places under the ocean. These deep places are known as oceanic **trenches**.

The Mariana Trench

The Mariana Trench is the deepest place on Earth. The deepest spot in the trench is called the *Challenger Deep*.

Naming Our World

We name the things in our world so we can talk with one another about them. This helps us work together and share what we know. When something is important to us, we may create new words to tell about it. We want to talk about it in every way that we can!

Landforms are important to us because Earth is important to us. We depend on Earth to live. We live in its mountains and valleys. We live near its oceans and in canyons high and low.

We love Earth and give its landforms many names. Of course, the best name for Earth is a simple one: we call it *home*.

Let's Do Science!

How are Earth's landforms alike and different? See for yourself!

What to Get

- 1 cup salt
- $1\frac{1}{2}$ cups water
- 4 cups flour
- measuring cup
- mixing bowl
- newspaper

What to Do

1 Lay the newspaper on a table or counter. Put a large mixing bowl on top of the newspaper.

2 Measure the right amounts of flour, water, and salt. Use your hands to mix everything together in the bowl.

3 Think of some landforms you have seen. Make them in the dough. Tell a friend what makes them each alike and different.

Glossary

canyons—flat areas surrounded by mountains with steep sides

climate—the usual type of weather a place gets

elevation—a measure of how high a place is

peaks—the highest points of mountains

plateaus—large, flat areas of land that are higher than other areas of surrounding land

ridges—long areas of land that are on top of mountains or hills

slope—the upward or downward slant of a landform

steep—almost straight up and down

trenches—long, narrow holes in the ocean floor

Index

Your Turn!

Land Art

Look at a map that shows landforms. Find any landform described in this book on the map. Think about what that real landform would look like. Use the map to help you. Then, draw a picture of the landform as you think it may look.